Chipmunk Family

Lois Brunner Bastian

A Wildlife Conservation Society Book

Franklin Watts
A Division of Grolier Publishing
New York • London • Hong Kong • Sydney
Danbury, Connecticut

The Wildlife Conservation Society (WCS) is dedicated to protecting and promoting the world's wildlife and wilderness areas. Founded in 1895 as the New York Zoological Society, the organization operates the Bronx Zoo, New York Aquarium, Central Park Wildlife Center, Queens Wildlife Center, and Prospect Park Wildlife Center. WCS also operates St. Catherines Wildlife Center, which is located off the coast of Georgia. The scientists at this center raise and study a variety of threatened and endangered animals.

WCS currently sponsors more than 350 field projects in 52 countries. The goal of these projects is to save wild landscapes and the animals that depend on them. In addition, WCS's pioneering environmental education programs reach more than 3 million students in the New York metropolitan area and are used in all 50 states and 14 foreign nations.

For my husband, Edward D. Bastian

Content Consultant: Kathy Carlstead, National Zoological Park, Smithsonian Institution, Washington, D. C.

Visit Franklin Watts on the Internet at
http://publishing.grolier.com

Library of Congress Cataloging-in-Publication Data

Bastian, Lois Brunner.
Chipmunk family / by Lois Brunner Bastian.
    p. cm.– (Wildlife Conservation Society Books)
    Includes bibliographical references and index.
    Summary: The author observes a family of chipmunks and describes their daily activities, life cycle, and behavior.
        ISBN 0-531-11683-2 (lib. bdg.)   0-531-16524-8 (pbk.)
        1. Chipmunks—Juvenile literature. [1. Chipmunks.] I. Title.
QL737.R68B386   2000
599.36'4–dc21   99-38206

GROLIER
PUBLISHING
©2000 Franklin Watts, a Division of Grolier Publishing
All rights reserved. Published simultaneously in Canada.
Printed in the United States of America.
1 2 3 4 5 6 7 8 9 10 R 09 08 07 06 05 04 03 02 01 00

Contents

Meet the Author

Lois Brunner Bastian is a writer and photographer. Her articles and images have appeared in many newspapers and national magazines. Ms. Bastian was born in Bethlehem, Pennsylvania, and graduated from Moravian College. She now lives in Holmdel, New Jersey.

Ms. Bastian found her inspiration for *Chipmunk Family* right in her own backyard.

"Chipmunks bounded into my life when I moved to New Jersey more than 25 years ago. They lived in the woods near my home and often came into the yard. Eventually, I began to watch these appealing animals and tried to find their burrows. The more I watched them, the more fascinated I became. I wanted to learn all about them.

"At the library, I found *Chipmunk Portrait* by B. A. and H. K. Henisch. It was the first of many books and

Lois Brunner Bastian's Home Town

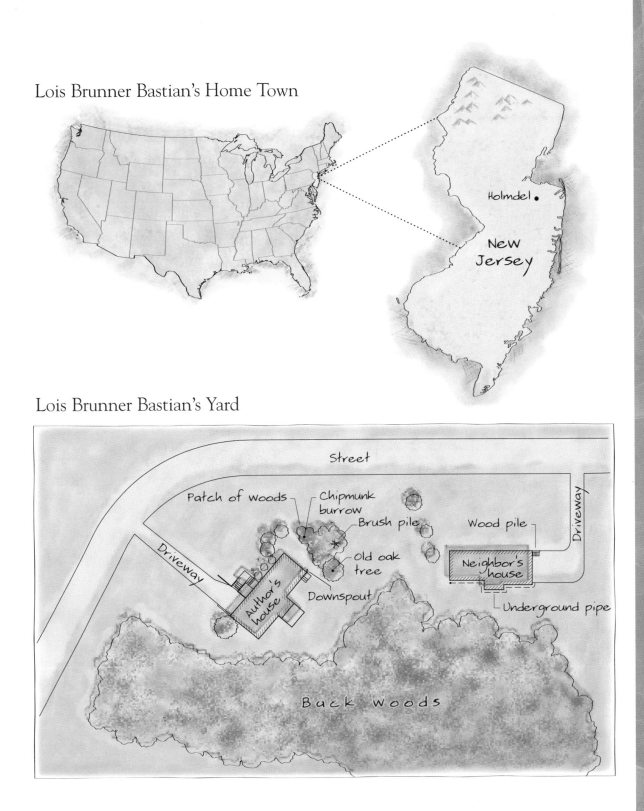

Holmdel •

New Jersey

Lois Brunner Bastian's Yard

Street

Patch of woods — Chipmunk burrow

Brush pile

Wood pile

Driveway

Driveway

Old oak tree

Neighbor's house

Author's house

Downspout

Underground pipe

B u c k   w o o d s

Lois Brunner Bastian kept careful notes about the chipmunks she watched. This page from her journal describes everything she observed during a 1-week period.

magazine articles I read on the subject. These resources were interesting, but they contained very little information about the day-to-day behavior of young chipmunks.

"Over the years, I watched several chipmunk litters grow up in my yard. On some days I watched them with friends or my husband, Edward. On other days, I watched them alone. Sometimes I observed them for up to 10 hours a day. During all those years, I kept detailed notes in my journal.

"At some point, I realized that I knew a great deal about young chipmunks. That's when I asked myself an important question: 'Should I write a book about a chipmunk family for young people?'

Ms. Bastian finally decided to write a manuscript. But before sending it to a publisher, she wanted an expert to look it over. She sent it to Dr. Lawrence Wishner, then a professor at Mary Washington College

Lois Brunner Bastian photographing a chipmunk

in Virginia and author of *Eastern Chipmunks: Secrets of Their Solitary Lives*. He checked the facts and encouraged Bastian to find a publisher.

Over the years, Ms. Bastain has also taken dozens of photographs of the chipmunks in her yard. Many of those photos appear in this book.

It is early spring, and this chipmunk has just emerged from its burrow.

Introduction

Early one morning, a female chipmunk scrambles along a tunnel that connects her *burrow* to the world above. When she reaches the plug of earth that seals the tunnel, she digs through it until daylight floods in from above.

First, she listens. Then, slowly, she pokes her nose out. A moment later, the rest of her head appears. Cautiously she looks around the patch of woods. Her eyes, ears, and nose tell her there is no danger. She dashes across the ground and rushes up an old oak tree. The oak tree grows in a patch of woods beside my house in New Jersey. In spite of the sharp cold of early March, the chipmunk's return to the outside world is a sign that spring will soon arrive.

When I see the chipmunk from my kitchen window, I hurry outside to get a closer look. Is she the female I have been watching for the last 4 years? I began to watch and keep notes about the chipmunks that spent time in my yard more than 20 years ago. During that time, I have kept track of seven females and their many litters.

Chipmunks are members of the squirrel family. They live in North America and northern Asia.

These lively neighbors are so appealing and so fascinating that I spend more time each year getting to know them. Some people go to faraway places like Africa to study lions, or to China to observe pandas. But as I have discovered, you can have a real-life adventure with a wild animal right in your own backyard.

Chipmunks often nose around in the woods.

Chapter 1

A Friend Returns

Chipmunks appear in the stories and legends of many Native American tribes. According to a Cherokee legend, the stripes on the chipmunk's back were made by a bear's claws.

Is the chipmunk beneath the oak tree really the one that spent so much time near the house last year? I can't tell by simply looking at her because all chipmunks that live in the eastern part of the United States and Canada look alike. Most adult chipmunks are about 6 inches (15 cm) long. The tail adds another 3 inches (7.5 cm). The fur on a chipmunk's head and shoulders is a blend of tan and gray. Its back and sides are a rich chestnut brown, and its underside is creamy white. What makes a chipmunk so striking are the black and white stripes down its back.

An eastern chipmunk has black and white stripes down its back and a long tail.

A downspout is a good place to hide from enemies.

Because a chipmunk is so small, it must be very cautious. Snakes, raccoons, foxes, rats, house cats, hawks, owls, and weasels are all enemies. A chipmunk's only defense is a safe hiding place. Whenever the chipmunks around my house sense danger, they dart into a downspout—a metal pipe that carries rain from the roof to the ground. The downspout is too narrow for most *predators* to enter.

The only way I can identify the chipmunk under the oak tree is to learn the location of her burrow. The chipmunks I've known dig a new front door for their burrow each spring. It's usually close to the entrance they used the year before. To find the burrow, I have to keep watching.

The next day, the chipmunk busily gathers sunflower seeds that have fallen from the bird feeder onto the lawn. She fills the pouches in her cheeks with the sunflower seeds and carries them back to the burrow.

As the chipmunk runs back to her burrow with the food, I watch carefully. The entrance to her burrow is only about 2 inches (5 cm) across, and it is about 12 inches (30 cm) from the one she used last year. So this is the same chipmunk I have been watching for 4 years! How wonderful to have her back! Without chipmunks, life would be far less interesting.

This chipmunk's cheek pouches bulge with seeds.

A male chipmunk zooms down the trunk of an oak tree.

The Female Chipmunk Chooses a Mate

The female chipmunk is not alone in the yard for long. A wildly active male soon appears. He zooms up and down the oak tree. He races in and out of the back woods behind my house. When he spots a squirrel sitting quietly on the lawn, he charges! He hits the squirrel smack in the belly and then dashes away. Chipmunks and squirrels don't usually attack one another, but during mating season, male chipmunks are full of spunk.

At first, the female chipmunk ignores the male. When a second male arrives, a wild chase begins. For nearly an hour, all three chipmunks streak across the lawn, speed through the back woods, and race up and down trees. They make soft squeaking noises as they run. Each male is trying to drive off the other so he can mate with the female.

Suddenly, the chase stops. The animals have disappeared, and all is quiet. Then, a few moments later, a racket breaks out in the downspout. All three chipmunks are jammed inside! Their bodies shake and bang against the pipe as they try to move in the cramped space. Their sharp claws screech against the metal like fingernails on a chalkboard. They let out shrill squeaks.

The female shoots out of the downspout. One of the males darts after her and follows her into a large hollow in the old oak tree. The female chooses him as

A male and female chipmunk leave a hollow in the oak tree.

her mate. The male and female stay inside the tree for about 30 minutes. Each time the other male tries to enter the hollow, the first one chases him away.

When the pair leaves the oak and returns to the downspout, a cold rain is falling. About 30 minutes later, the female returns to her burrow, and the male disappears into the back woods.

Male and female chipmunks come together only to mate. In central New Jersey, mating usually occurs in March and again in late June through mid-July. The rest of the year, males and females live separate lives. Mating doesn't always produce young chipmunks. When it does, the babies are born about 31 days after mating.

I look at my calendar and see that the female in my yard should give birth around April 13. The newborns usually stay inside their mother's burrow for about 6 weeks. That means I will probably see the babies in the last week of May. I can hardly wait!

Chipmunks often pause and look around, checking for danger.

Chapter 3

The Babies Are Born

During the next few weeks, the female leaves her burrow nearly every day. She noses about and gathers food. Sometimes other chipmunks wander into the yard looking for seeds that have fallen out of the bird feeder.

Chipmunks are *territorial* animals. Whenever the female spies another chipmunk in her area, she chases it away. The *intruder* usually backs off, but sometimes a fight breaks out.

As mid-April draws closer, the female seems nervous. After a heavy snow, I look for her tracks on the ground, but there are none. She doesn't leave the burrow for several days.

When she finally comes out, it's only for a few minutes. She digs through the dirt and leaves in search of tender shoots of grass, oak bark, and young dandelion leaves. These foods aren't usually part of her diet. She licks a brick, too. She needs the *minerals* it contains.

A chipmunk digs through leaves and dirt in search of a tasty treat.

A mother chipmunk has four pairs of nipples to nurse her young.

The female chipmunks I've watched behaved like this only when they were nursing their young. This must mean her babies have been born. Imagine tiny newborn chipmunks with no teeth or hair! Each one is probably curled up in a tight ball with its eyes and ears closed.

When the female stands up on her back legs, I see eight faint spots in the white fur on her underside. These spots are nipples. The babies suck their mother's milk from them. The nipples prove that the babies have been born. The female chipmunk is a mother.

At birth, chipmunk babies are about the size of a bumblebee. When they are 15 days old, their bodies are about 3 inches (7.5 cm) long.

The female will raise her young inside the burrow until they are old enough to care for themselves. In about 6 weeks, the young chipmunks will be scurrying about the yard. I wonder how big the *litter* is. How many baby chipmunks are curled up inside the burrow?

At first, the female spends most of her time caring for her young. Then she begins to leave the burrow for longer periods of time. On one trip, she runs to a pipe in a neighbor's yard. She climbs inside it and disappears. After that, she goes to the pipe often, but I can't figure out why. Where does the pipe go? How does she get out? It takes weeks to solve this mystery.

As her young grow, they don't need to be fed so often. Soon the female chipmunk spends even more time outside. Sometimes she sits quietly beside the entrance to the burrow for an hour at a time. She seems to be taking a break from the demands of her litter.

A chipmunk may sit motionless for minutes at a time.

Two youngsters cautiously leave the burrow.

Chapter 4

The Young Chipmunks Appear

One morning in late May, a young chipmunk peeps out from the mouth of the burrow. A moment later, a second youngster joins the first one. When several crows caw loudly, the chipmunks disappear underground.

A few minutes later, two tiny noses inch into sight. Is it safe to come out? Little by little, the two young chipmunks emerge. They are about two-thirds adult size and look just like their mother. Wobbling on their back legs, they stand up and gaze all around. One loses its balance and topples onto all fours. Standing upright on two legs will take practice.

For the next 3 days, the two youngsters come out together for short periods. At first, I watch them from a distance. They examine every leaf, blade of grass, and twig near the hole. The shadow of a flying bird sends them fleeing underground. When tree leaves flutter in the wind, they crouch fearfully just inside the burrow's mouth. After watching for a long time, the young ones are finally satisfied that the fluttering leaves are no threat.

To photograph the chipmunk family, I sit about 36 inches (91 cm) from the burrow entrance for hours at a time—and for days on end. The mother is used to seeing me in the yard, so she is not afraid of me. Because she trusts me, the young chipmunks do, too. As long as I stay perfectly still, the chipmunks seem to think I am part of the landscape. At first, the click of my camera shutter startles them, but they soon get used to the sound.

As time passes, the young chipmunks grow bolder. They begin to explore the yard. They dig among fallen leaves, climb trees, and teeter on twigs too slender to hold them. Like most baby animals, they are very appealing and fun to watch.

When their mother is nearby, the two seem more daring. They follow her to the old oak tree. This is the farthest they have ever been from their burrow. After exploring the inside of the tree, they discover a brush pile—a heap of dead branches and twigs.

The young chipmunks examine everything around them.

The brush pile is a safe place to play.

This brush pile is like a jungle gym to young chipmunks. It is full of cozy pockets and hidden tunnels. They wriggle through it from side to side and then from top to bottom. Every now and then, they stop and sit on a branch. Best of all, the brush pile provides instant shelter in case of danger.

Day after day, I watched the two youngsters exploring the backyard. Was it always the same two chipmunks? There is no way to know. It is not unusual for some young to be stronger and bolder, while others are slower and more timid. I would have to wait for all the youngsters to leave the burrow at once to know how many there are.

One morning, I notice two little chipmunks sitting beside the burrow. An hour later, two more youngsters appear. An hour after that, a fifth young chipmunk joins them. Two of the youngsters head straight for the brush pile. The other three stay near the burrow, but soon they too dare to travel as far as the brush pile. All five stay within the patch of woods near the house.

Meanwhile, the female hurries back and forth between the lawn and the patch of woods. She lets the youngsters explore on their own, but now and then she scampers to the oak tree and the brush pile. She seems to be checking on them. When the young see her, they draw close—nose to nose—in what looks like a greeting or a kiss. They paw her, climb over her, hang onto her, and nibble her gently.

The youngsters try to cuddle with their mother.

See how the chipmunks' colors blend in with their surroundings.

All day long, the patch of woods is alive with busy little chipmunks. They dart in and out of the old oak tree, disappear into the brush pile, and then make a mad dash for the burrow. After a brief rest, they start up again.

It's impossible to keep track of them all. If I take my eyes off one for a second, it seems to disappear. That's because a chipmunk's colors blend in with the carpet of dry oak leaves on the ground.

In the late afternoon, the whole family returns to the burrow for the night. The next morning all five young chipmunks appear. Then, a few moments later, a sixth youngster comes out of the burrow. This is the largest litter the female chipmunk has ever had.

All these chipmunks are trying to use the burrow entrance at the same time.

The Chipmunks Grow Up

With a mother chipmunk and six youngsters rushing in and out of the burrow all day long, the entrance hole is growing larger. Still, when several chipmunks try to squeeze through at the same time, there is a traffic jam. Sometimes the youngsters startle one another, and one leaps straight up into the air.

While the youngsters explore, their mother gathers oak leaves. She selects each leaf carefully. It can't be too dry or too damp. The female holds each leaf in her mouth and folds it into a compact bundle with her front paws. It has to be small enough to fit through the burrow's entrance. Some of the leaves will be used as bedding, others will be used to cover the chipmunks' growing store of food. When a blue jay calls out, "Thief! Thief!" the young chipmunks shoot upright on their back legs, ears erect. After the bird flies off, one youngster chirps softly while it

A chipmunk folds an oak leaf into a bundle.

A chipmunk nibbles on a wild mushroom.

folds leaves and takes them into the burrow—just as its mother has done.

Each day, the chipmunks collect food. Nuts, seeds, and fruit make up a chipmunk's main diet. They may also eat worms, snails, and mushrooms. They may even munch on insects—such as the crunchy brown beetle I once saw a chipmunk eat, headfirst, one bite at a time. The youngsters drink water from small puddles that have formed in fallen leaves and in the hollows of rocks.

Chipmunks eat soft foods, such as berries and mushrooms, right away. They usually store only hard foods, such as nuts and seeds, underground. A chipmunk's urge to store food is intense. No matter how full its storeroom, the animal continues to collect more.

When it gathers acorns and other large nuts, a chipmunk bites off any sharp stems and then tucks one nut into each cheek pouch. Fitting a nut into a cheek pouch can take a lot of effort, and placing odd-shaped nuts in its mouth can be a real challenge. It is amusing to watch the animal reposition a nut—again and again—until it fits comfortably. The chipmunk then grabs a third nut between its teeth and carries its load back to its burrow.

After eating anything wet or sticky, a chipmunk washes itself. First, it moistens its front paws with its tongue, then it rubs its paws over its face and mouth.

A chipmunk *grooms* its entire body several times a day. To clean its tail, the animal pulls it—from the base to the tip—through its mouth and over its tongue. To clean hard-to-reach spots, the animal bends, stretches, and twists itself into comical positions.

After 9 days of exploring, the youngsters are familiar with the patch of woods, the lawn, and the downspout. One youngster stays close to home, but the other five spend most of their time away from the burrow. All day long, they dart across the yard and dig in the soil. One daredevil scampers high up in a swaying birch tree.

This chipmunk is grooming.

Youngsters practice the hold that adult males use when mating.

As the young chipmunks run across the yard, one youngster comes up behind another and grabs it tightly around the middle with its forepaws. They are playing, but it's an effective hold. The captive struggles to pull away, dragging the first one behind, until it finally breaks free. This is the way a male grasps a female during mating.

Suddenly, the mother chipmunk shrills a sharp cry. Danger! All games stop instantly. The youngsters closest to the burrow dive in. The rest freeze in place while their mother drives off an intruding chipmunk.

When the excitement is over, the mother comes back to the burrow, stands tall on her back legs and begins to "sing." Her loud, shrill, rhythmic chirps mixed with trills sound like a bird's call. Her song lasts

A chipmunk explores the neighbor's woodpile.

about 3 minutes. It begins slowly, getting faster and louder until it reaches a *crescendo*. Then it tapers off to a few after-chirps. During the mother's song, the young sit calmly beside her.

Most of the time, the young chipmunks stay fairly close to the burrow, but sometimes they tag along behind their mother when she travels farther. One day, the female and two youngsters run into the neighbor's yard, and they all disappear into the pipe I have been wondering about.

A few moments later, the chipmunks appear near the neighbor's driveway and dart into a woodpile. It turns out that the pipe runs underground along the entire length of the neighbor's house. In the woodpile, the chipmunks disappear then reappear, poking their heads in and out of holes between the pieces of firewood.

At last, the mystery is solved. The chipmunks use the pipe to cross the neighbor's yard without being seen.

Two youngsters learn how to fight.

Chapter 6

The Chipmunks Leave Home

After 12 days, most of the young spend hours on their own. I see one climbing up the inside of the downspout. Another travels completely around my house—hugging the foundation wall all the way.

Most of the time, the animals travel close to a building or the edge of the woods so that predators can't spot them. When crossing exposed areas, such as the lawn, they run at top speed. Both adults and youngsters seem to have a good sense of direction.

Now the young spend less time playing together. One chipmunk sits beside the burrow and nips another as it tries to come out. The chipmunk squeals and retreats underground.

The young chipmunks are no longer interested in following their mother. They listen closely to the calls of distant chipmunks. When their mother sings, one youngster joins in with soft chirps—creating a chipmunk duet.

By mid-June, the young seem frightened when they are near their mother. They hold their heads low, as if they are afraid. In the mid-afternoon, one youngster returns to the burrow. The mother nips the youngster

A youngster tries to dive into the burrow.

as it dives into the burrow. When a second youngster arrives, the mother tries to chase it away. A third youngster ducks into the burrow when the mother leaves.

When the mother returns, she enters the burrow. An hour later, a fourth youngster darts into the burrow, but the tip of its tail remains outside. Soon the youngster comes back out. Its head is covered with loose soil. The female chipmunk has plugged the burrow's entrance with soil to keep the youngsters out.

The youngster digs frantically, trying to get inside. As it digs, it makes soft clucking sounds. Its tail jerks back and forth rapidly. The fifth youngster has the same trouble. They dig together, but they can't get into the burrow. By nipping and chasing them earlier that afternoon, she was warning them. They are no longer welcome.

As they creep off to the brush pile, the little chipmunks seem bewildered. The last youngster straggles home at 5:30 P.M., tries three times to dig its way in, and then gives up. At 6:30 P.M., one youngster perches alone on the brush pile.

This young chipmunk has been shut out of the burrow. It sits alone on the brush pile.

The mother chipmunk zooms down the oak tree to chase a youngster away.

When a chipmunk digs a burrow, it removes the soil through a work tunnel that is later sealed. As a result, there is no disturbed soil near the burrow opening, so it is hard for predators to spot.

Why did the female allow some youngsters inside, and not others? I don't know for sure. Perhaps the chipmunks that stayed out later in the day are ready to care for themselves.

The next morning, the entrance is open again and the mother is out. Nevertheless, the youngsters in the patch of woods keep their distance. The mother stays close to the burrow most of the day, as if to keep them from returning. She nips the youngsters that are still allowed in the burrow. Is she warning them that they, too, must leave soon?

In the afternoon, the mother blocks the burrow's entrance again. It is still plugged the next morning. When one young chipmunk heads toward it, the mother swoops down a tree trunk and frightens the youngster away.

The burrow is closed, but the mother is outside. How can that be? Later, when the mother is away, the same youngster returns to nose around. It makes a surprising discovery—the mother has dug a new front door about 12 inches (30 cm) away from the first one. The youngster streaks into the burrow like a shot.

In the early afternoon, the female chipmunk returns to the burrow with some nuts. It takes her a few seconds to wriggle through the snug, new open-

ing. When a youngster arrives an hour later, both the new and the old entrances are blocked. The homeless chipmunks stay in the brush pile for the rest of the day. They don't seem to know what else to do. Soon they will go off on their own and make their own burrows.

This mother is having a lot of trouble getting her litter to leave home. This isn't always the case. Some youngsters leave willingly just 10 days to 2 weeks after they first come aboveground. Others need only a few nips from their mother before setting out on their own.

As the mother sits at her new front door the next afternoon, a youngster comes out of the burrow. They sit together peacefully. Oddly enough, this young chipmunk is still allowed to stay in the burrow.

The mother runs across the yard, drinks some water trapped in the downspout, and wipes her wet chin on the grass. When she returns to the burrow, the stay-at-home youngster playfully grabs her around the middle. Surprisingly, its mother doesn't object. The two chipmunks go underground for the night.

During the next few days, several of the other young chipmunks come into the yard from the back woods. When the mother and her young meet, she chases them, and they chase each other. Now they are rivals, rather than relatives.

Only this youngster is still allowed in the burrow.

As time passes, the youngsters come back to the yard less and less often. The female's life is peaceful once more. Each young chipmunk has its own territory, and has built its own burrow. The youngsters have grown used to caring for themselves.

In early July, the female mates again. By mid-September, another chipmunk family romps around in the patch of woods in my yard. A few weeks later the new youngsters head off on their own—just like their older brothers and sisters.

In early autumn, a second litter of chipmunks scurries through the woods.

In the winter, a chipmunk curls up and naps in its burrow.

In late October, the female chipmunk goes underground and closes the mouth of her burrow. She settles down for the winter on a bed of oak leaves. During winter, the chipmunk stirs occasionally and eats from her store of food. Sometimes she leaves her burrow briefly—even when there is snow on the ground.

Chipmunks sometimes come above ground in the middle of winter.

When March arrives, the chipmunk wakes up, digs a new entrance, and takes her first breath of spring. Another chipmunk season has begun.

Important Words

burrow (noun) an underground hole that an animal lives in

crescendo (noun) a gradual increase in the volume of a sound

groom (verb) when an animal cleans its own body

intruder (noun) an animal that forces its way into a place where it is unwelcome

litter (noun) several animals born at one time to one mother

mineral (noun) a chemical substance, such as rock or ore, that occurs in nature

predator (noun) an animal that hunts other animals for food

territorial (adjective) describes an animal that claims an area for itself

To Find Out More

Books   Boring, Mel and Linda Garrow. *Rabbits, Squirrels and Chipmunks*. New York: Gareth Stevens Publishing, 1998.

Burton, John A., Jim Channell, and Angela Royston. *Mammals of North America*. New York: Silver Dolphin, 1995.

Grassy, John and Charles I. Keene. *Mammals* (National Audubon First Field Guide). New York: Scholastic, 1998.

Miller, Sara Swan. *Rodents: From Mice to Muskrats*. Danbury, CT: Franklin Watts, 1998.

Tony, Dr. Hare and Allison Warner. *Animal Fact-File: Head-to-Tail Profiles of over 90 Mammals*. New York: Facts on File, 1999.

Tunis, Edwin. *Chipmunks on the Doorstep*. New York: Thomas Y. Crowell Company, 1971.

Video   *Chipmunks*. Nature Watch. TV Ontario, 1988.

Chipmunk

http://www.cws-scf.ec.gc.ca/hww-fap/chipmunk/chipmunk.html

This site features all kinds of information about chipmunks and a map that shows where different kinds of chipmunks live.

The Chipmunk Page

http://monticello.avenue.gen.va.us/Community/Environ/EnvironEdCenter/Habitat/AnimalStudy/Mammal/Chipmunk.html

This site was developed by the Environmental Education Center in Charlottesville, Virginia. It describes what chipmunks look like, where they live, what they eat, and more.

The Chipmunk Place

http://www.owca.com/

Learn about different kinds of chipmunks, see stunning photos, and read some fun facts about famous chipmunks.

National Park Service

Office of Public Inquiries

P.O. Box 37127

Washington, DC 20013

Wildlife Conservation Society

http://www.wcs.org

2300 Southern Blvd.

Bronx, NY 10460-1099

Index

Photographs© : Animals Animals: 43 (Breck P. Kent); ENP Images: 18 (Steve Gettle); Lois Brunner Bastian: 7 (E. D. Bastian), cover, 6, 8, 12, 13, 16, 20, 22, 24, 25, 26, 27, 28, 29, 30, 32, 33, 34, 36, 37, 38, 41, 42; Photo Researchers: 14 (Nick Bergkessel), 10 (E. R. Degginger), 11 (Anthony Mercieca), 44 (Gregory K. Scott); Photodisc, Inc.: margins, background; Visuals Unlimited: 31 (Gary W. Carter); Wildlife Collection: 19, 21 (Tom Vezo).

LAKE COUNTY PUBLIC LIBRARY
INDIANA

Some materials may be renewable by phone or in person if there are
no reserves or fines due.   www.lakeco.lib.in.us   LCP#0390